SUPER MAZES
FOR KIDS

EASY, Medium, and Difficult Mazes for Children

written by

Peter I. Kattan
and
Nicola I. Kattan

www.PetraBooks.com

www.PetraBooks.com

Ordering Information:
Quantity sales. Special discounts are available on quantity purchases by corporations, associations. Orders by U.S. trade bookstores and wholesalers. Please visit www.PetraBooks.com

Printed in the United States of America

ISBN-13: 979-8-8692-0452-3

1
SUPER EASY

2
Super Easy

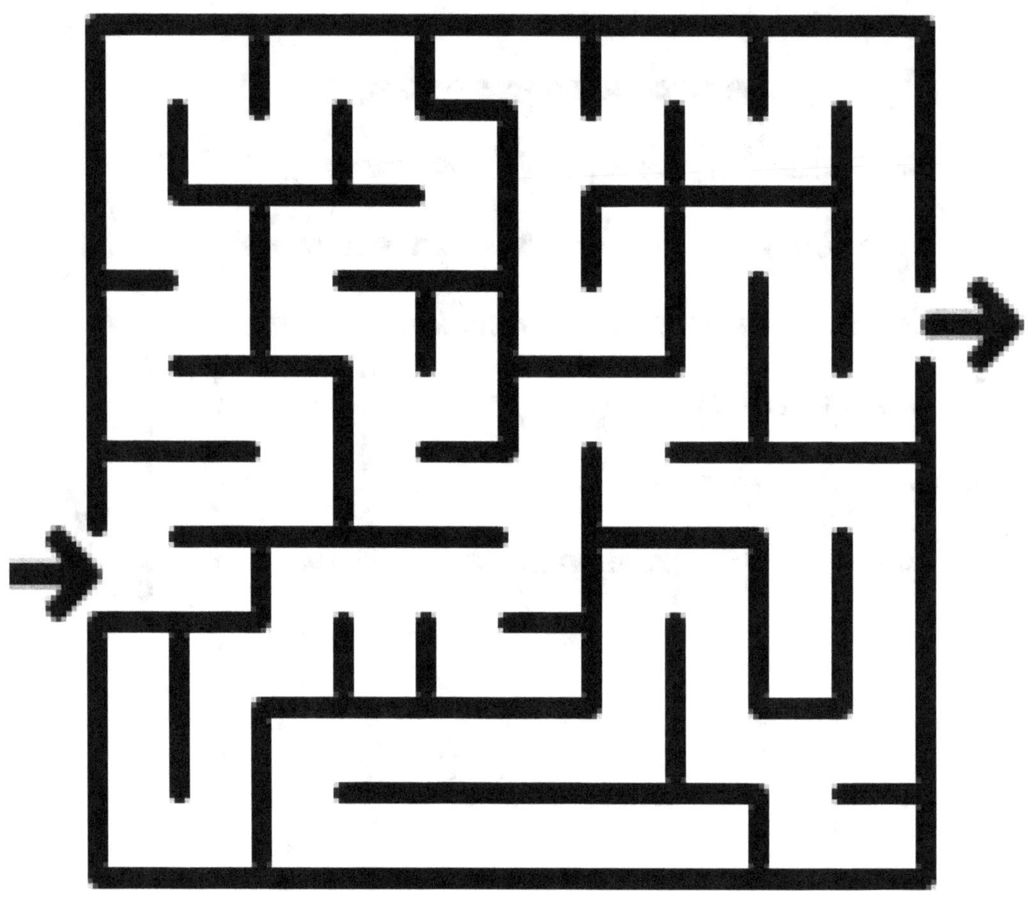

3
Super Easy

4
Super Easy

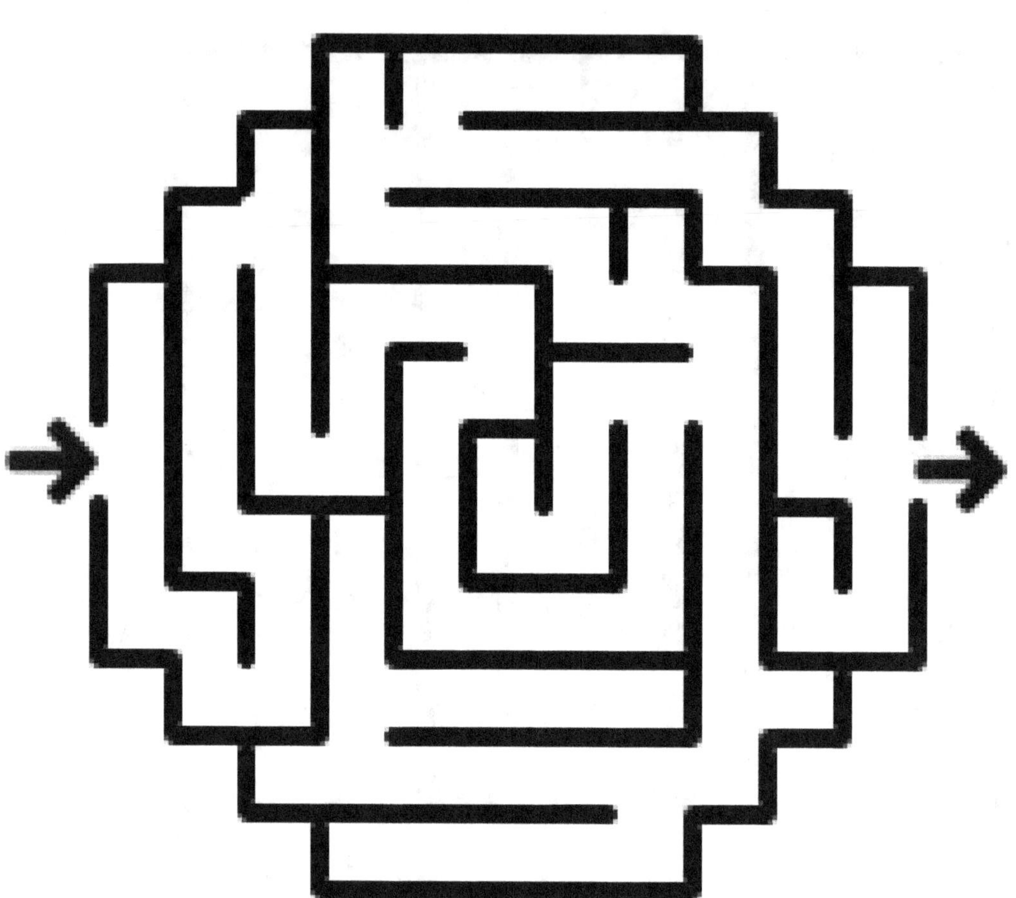

5
Super Easy

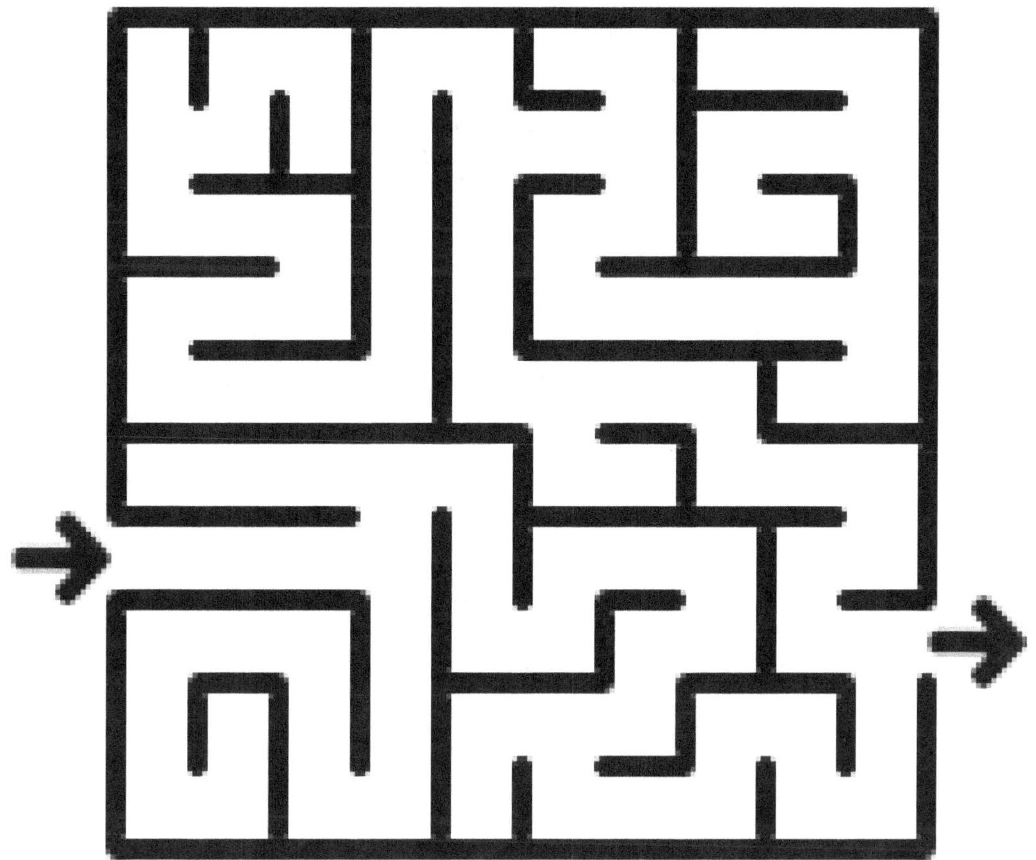

6
Super Easy

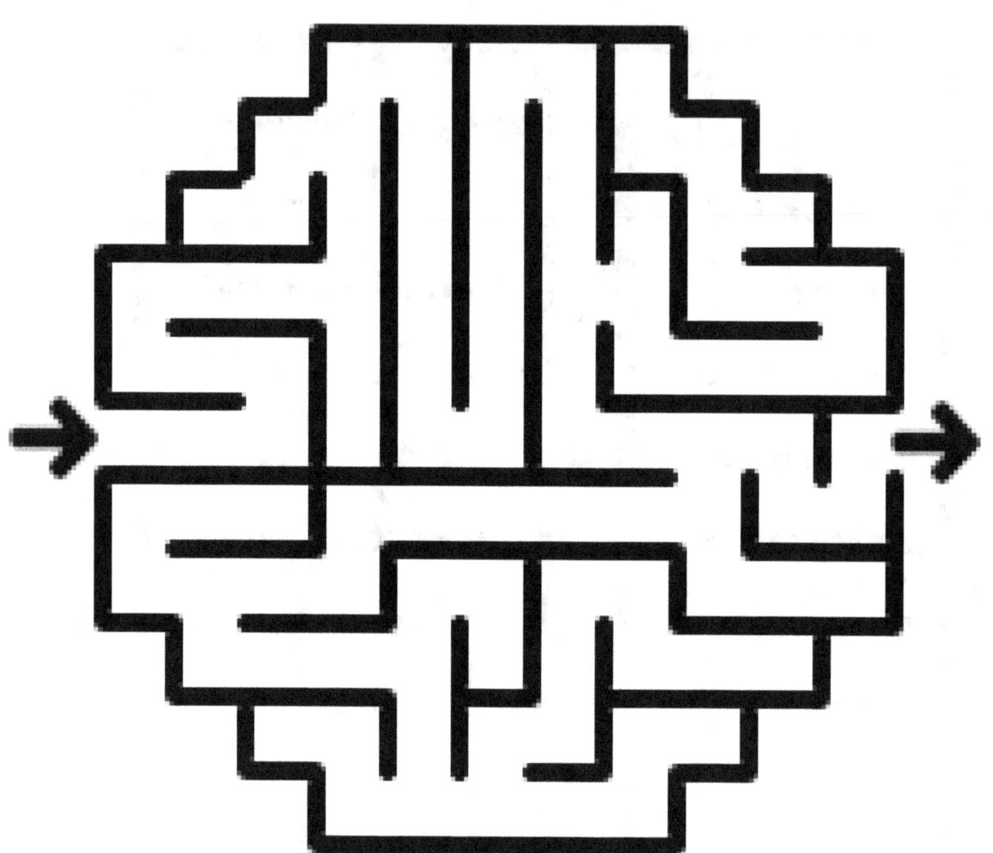

7
Super Easy

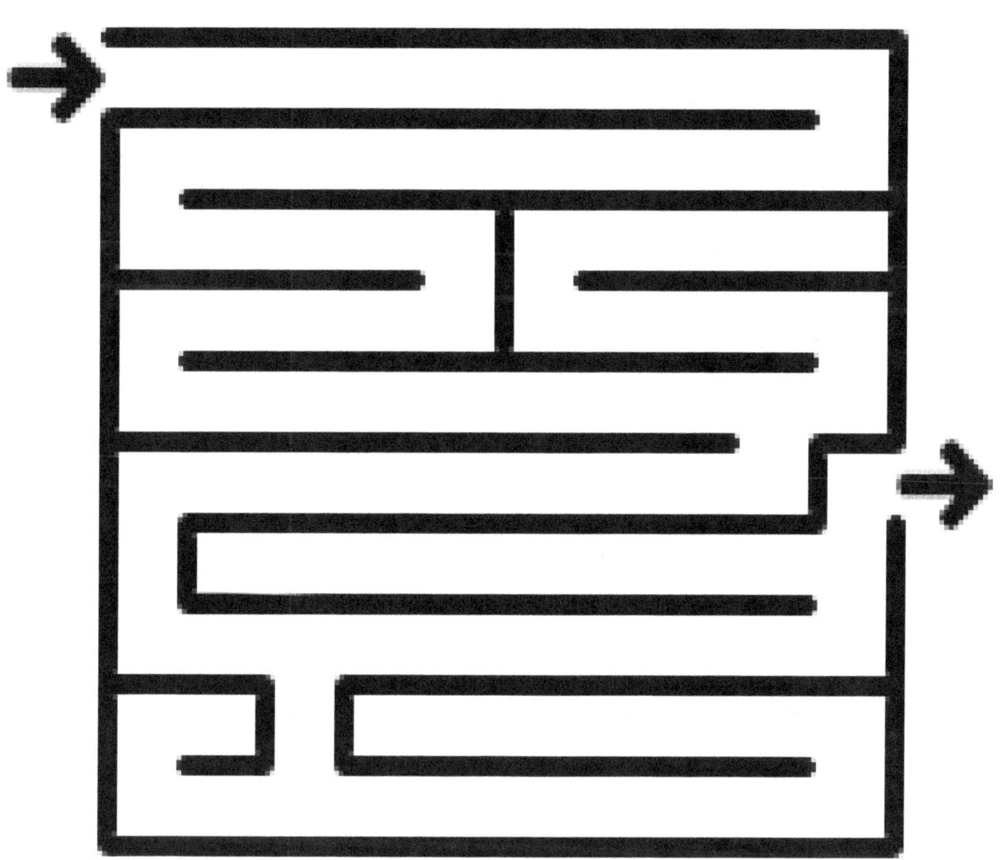

8
Super Easy

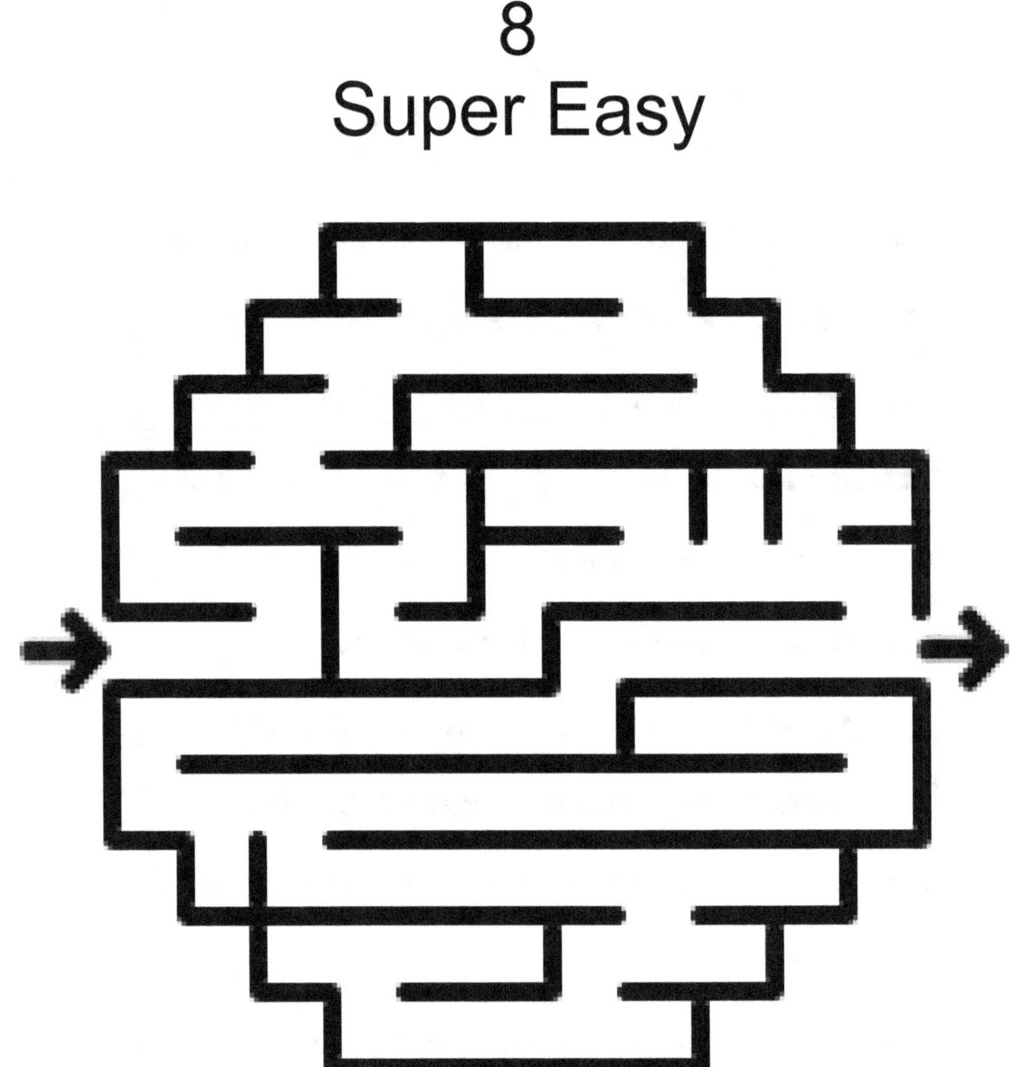

9
Super Easy

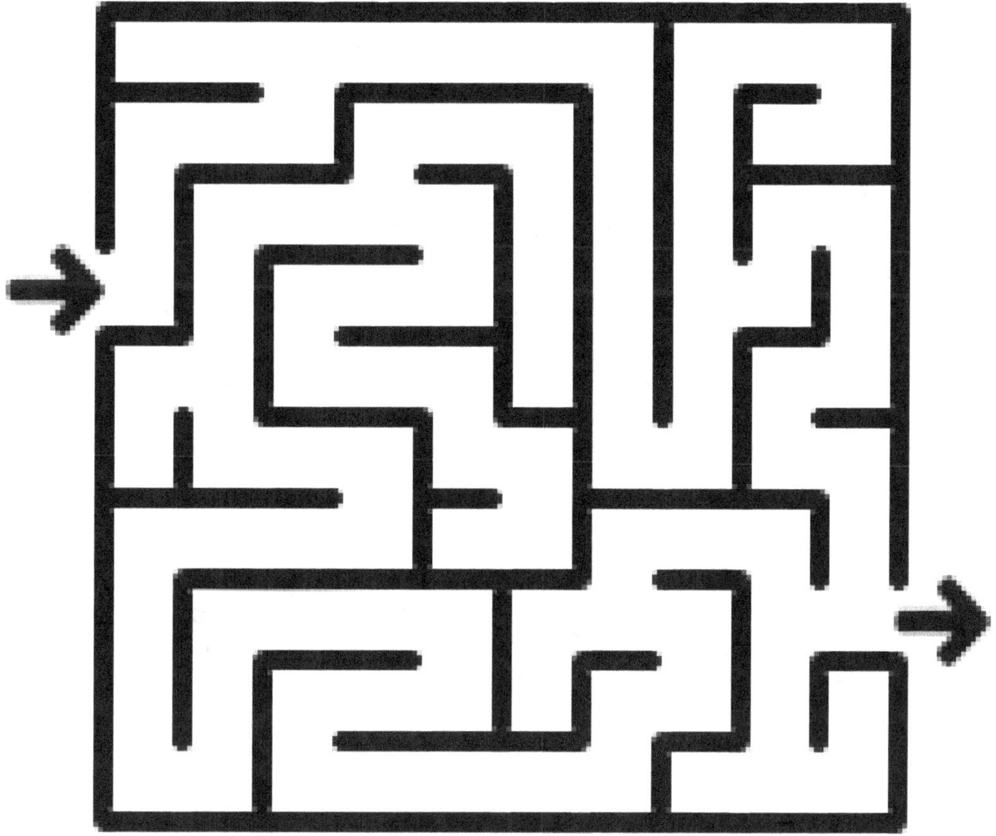

10
Super Easy

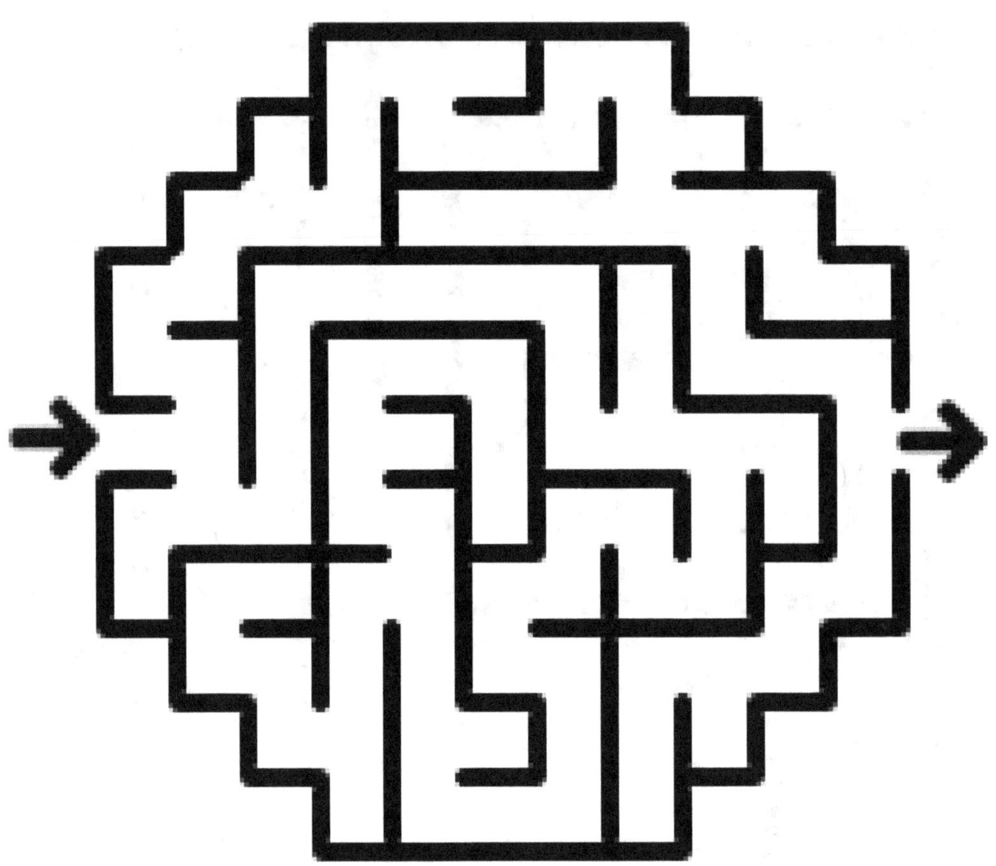

11
Easy

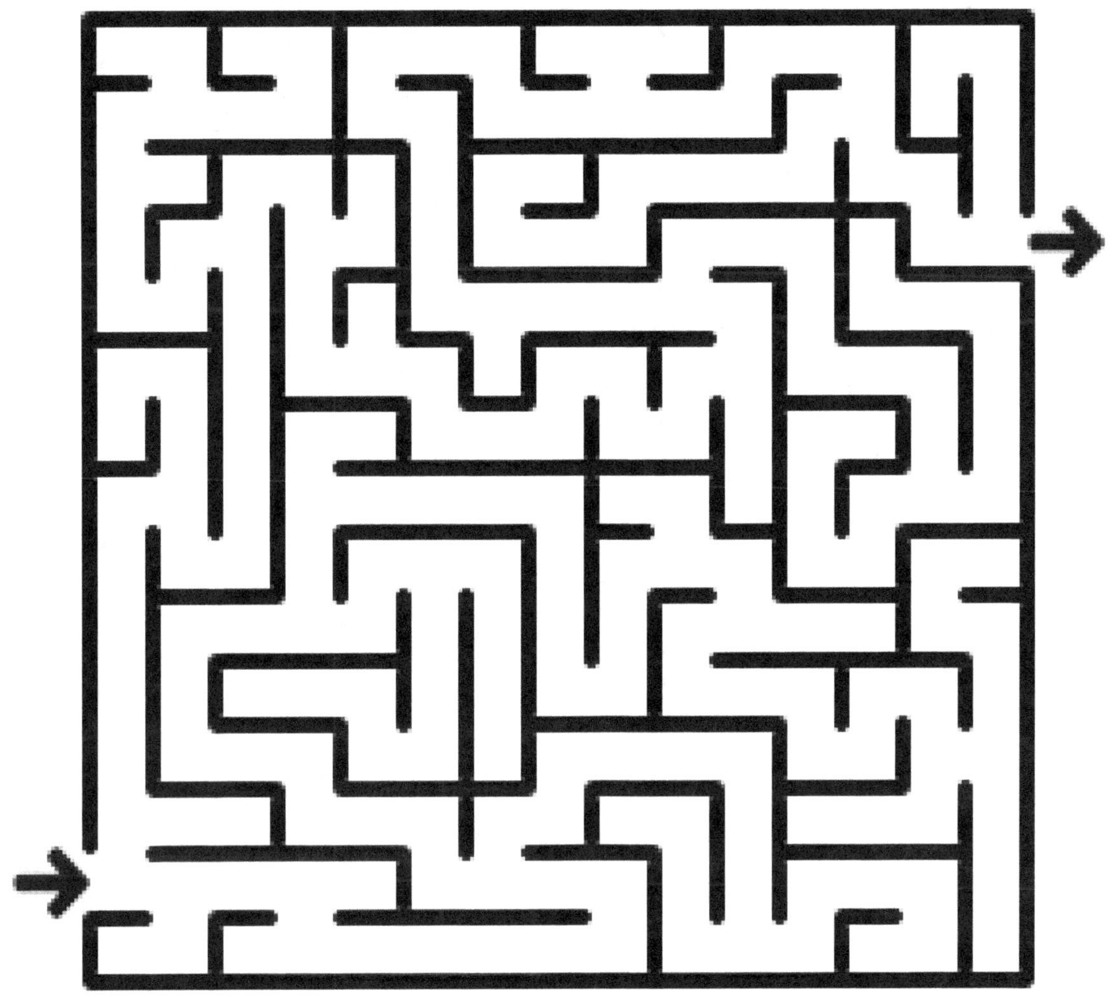

12
Easy

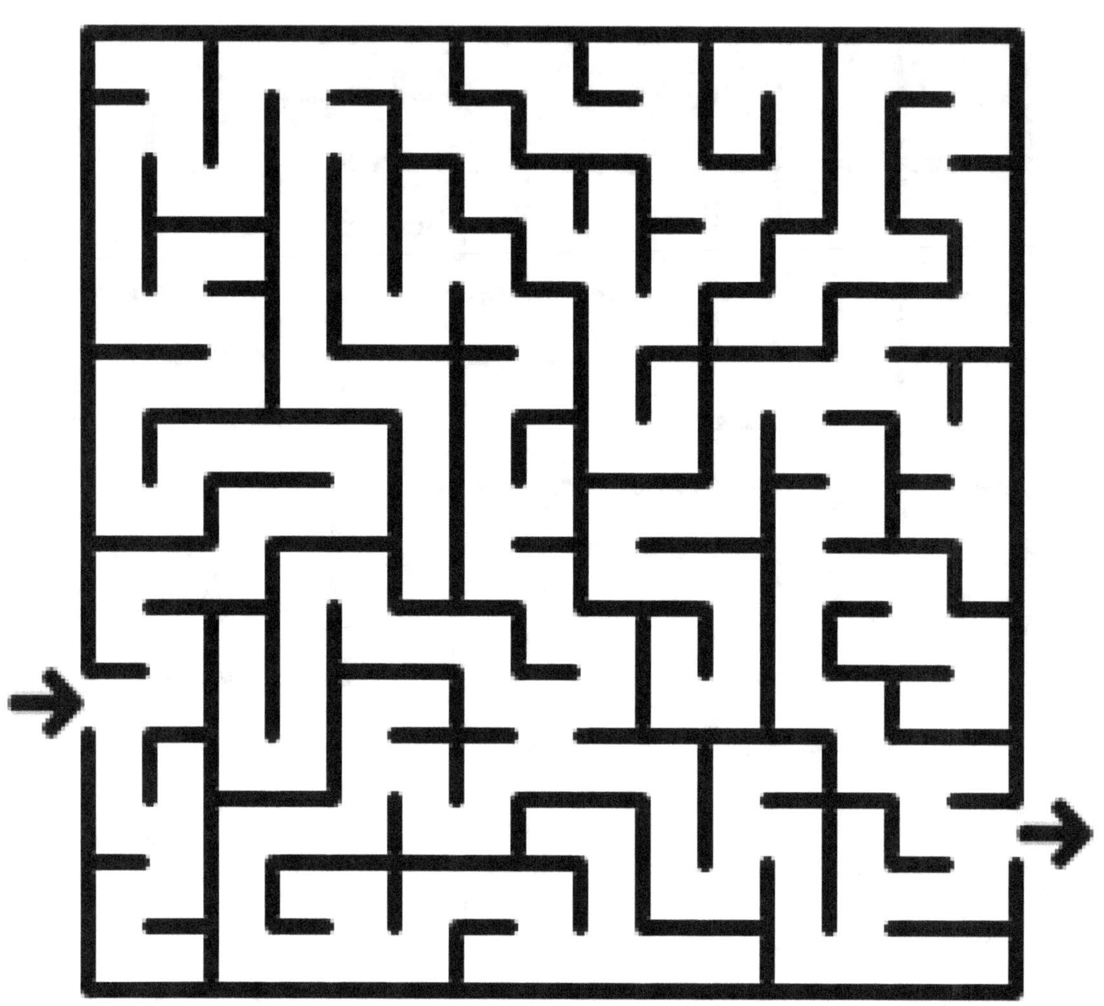

13
Easy

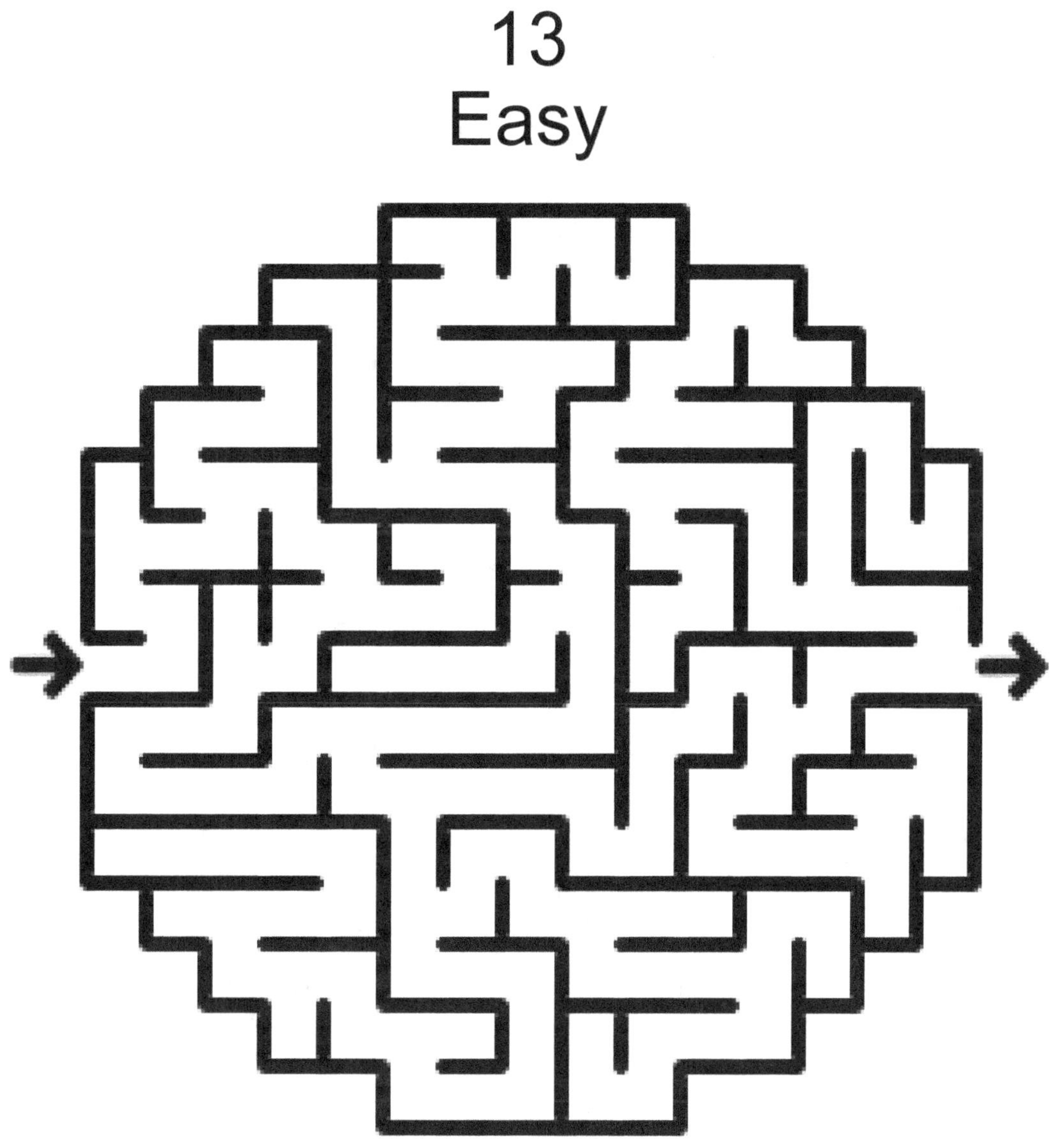

14
Easy

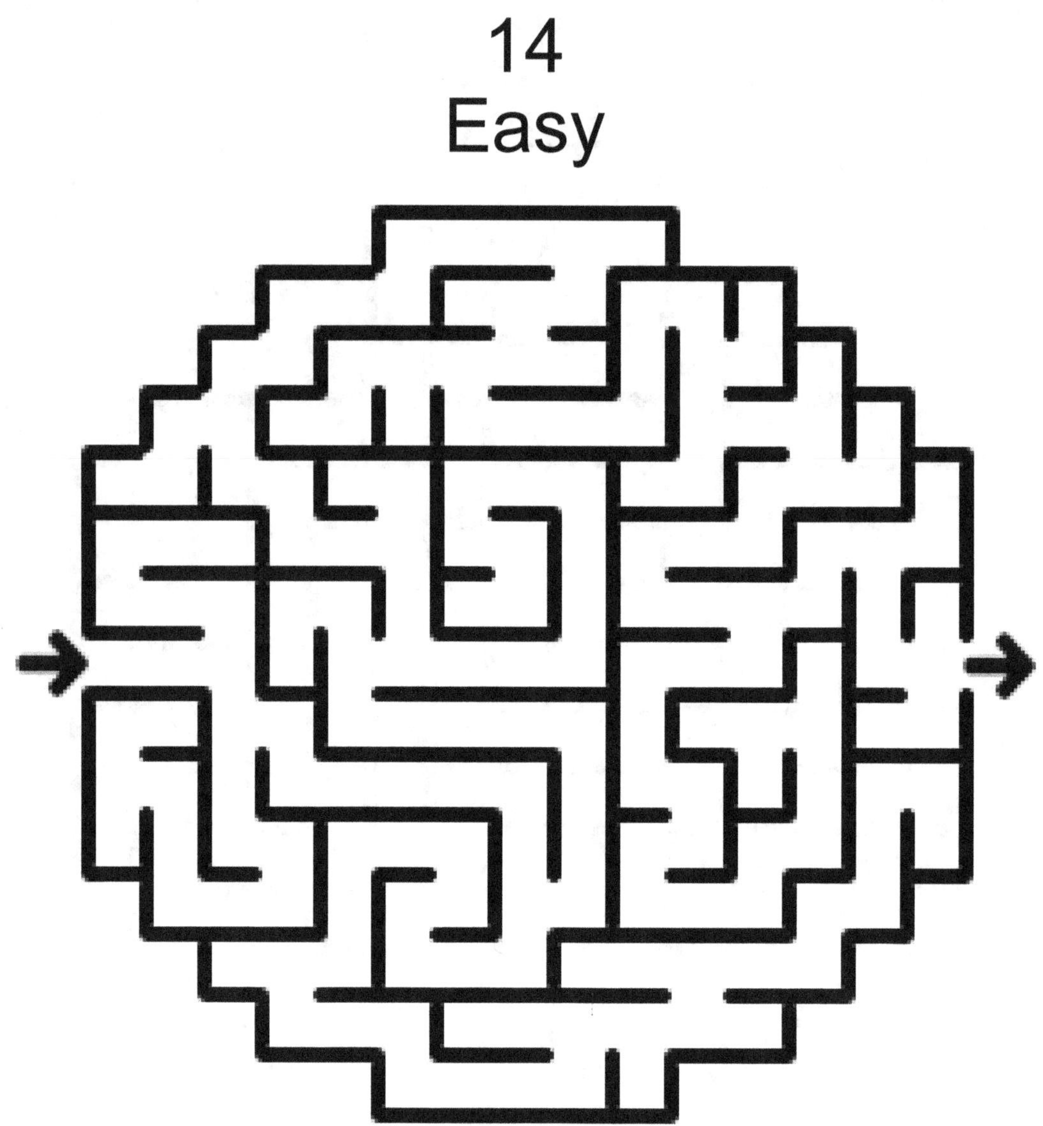

15
Easy

16
Easy

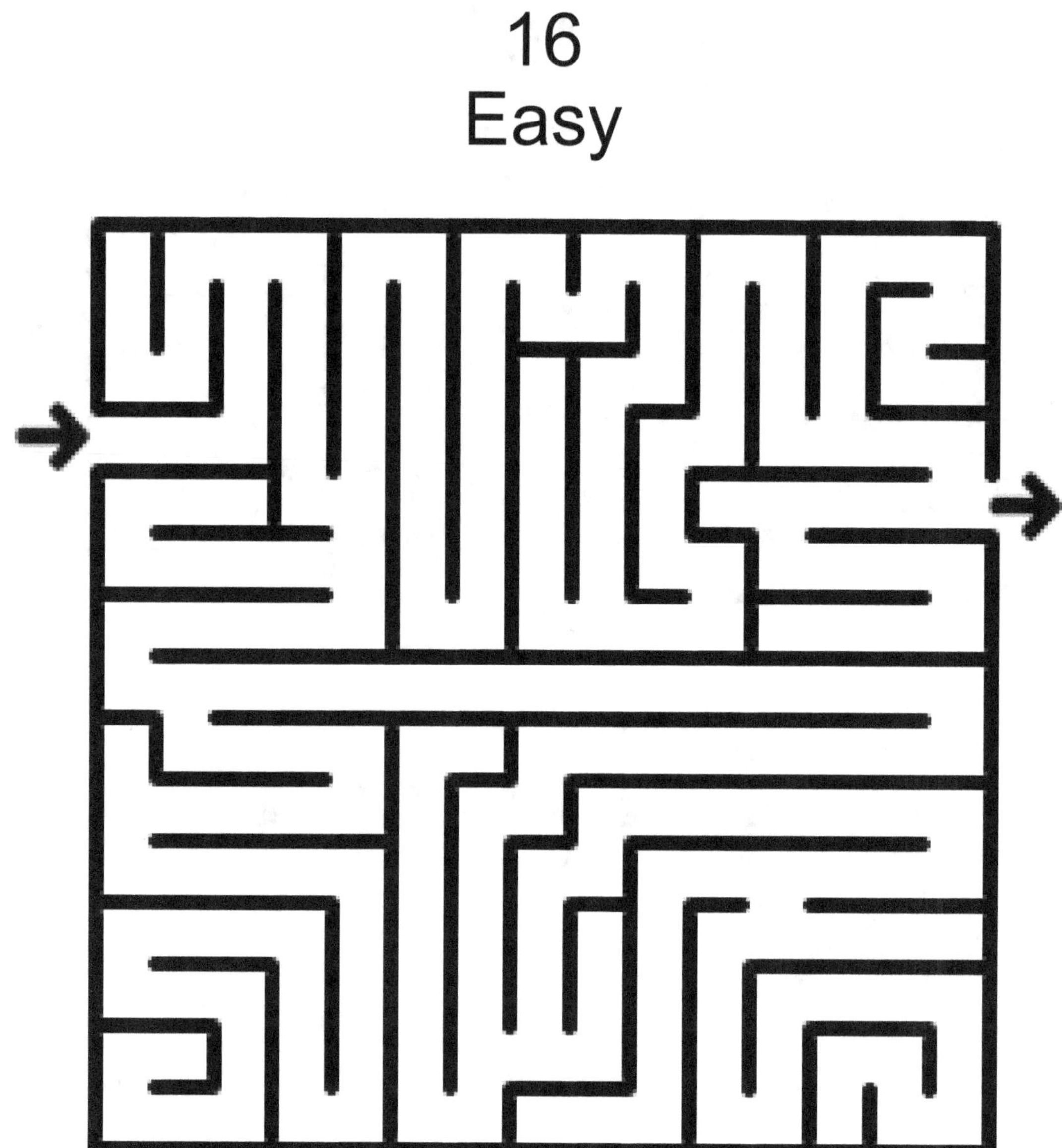

17
Easy

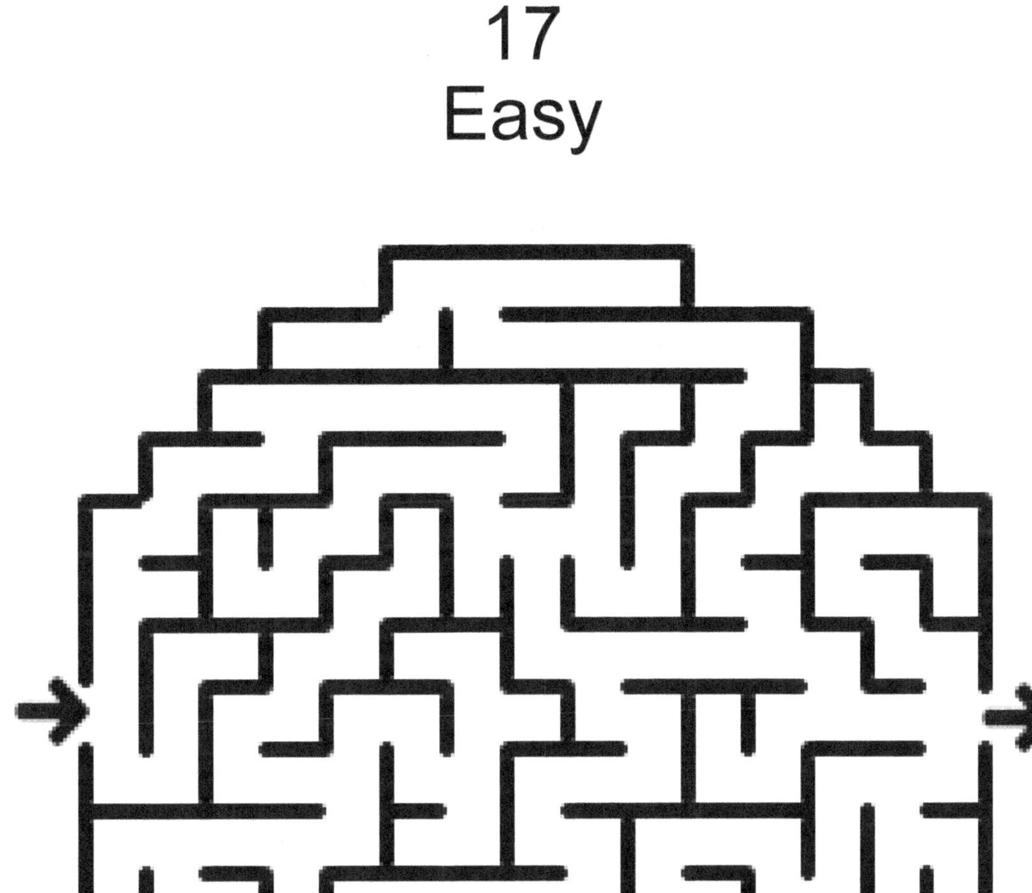

18
Easy

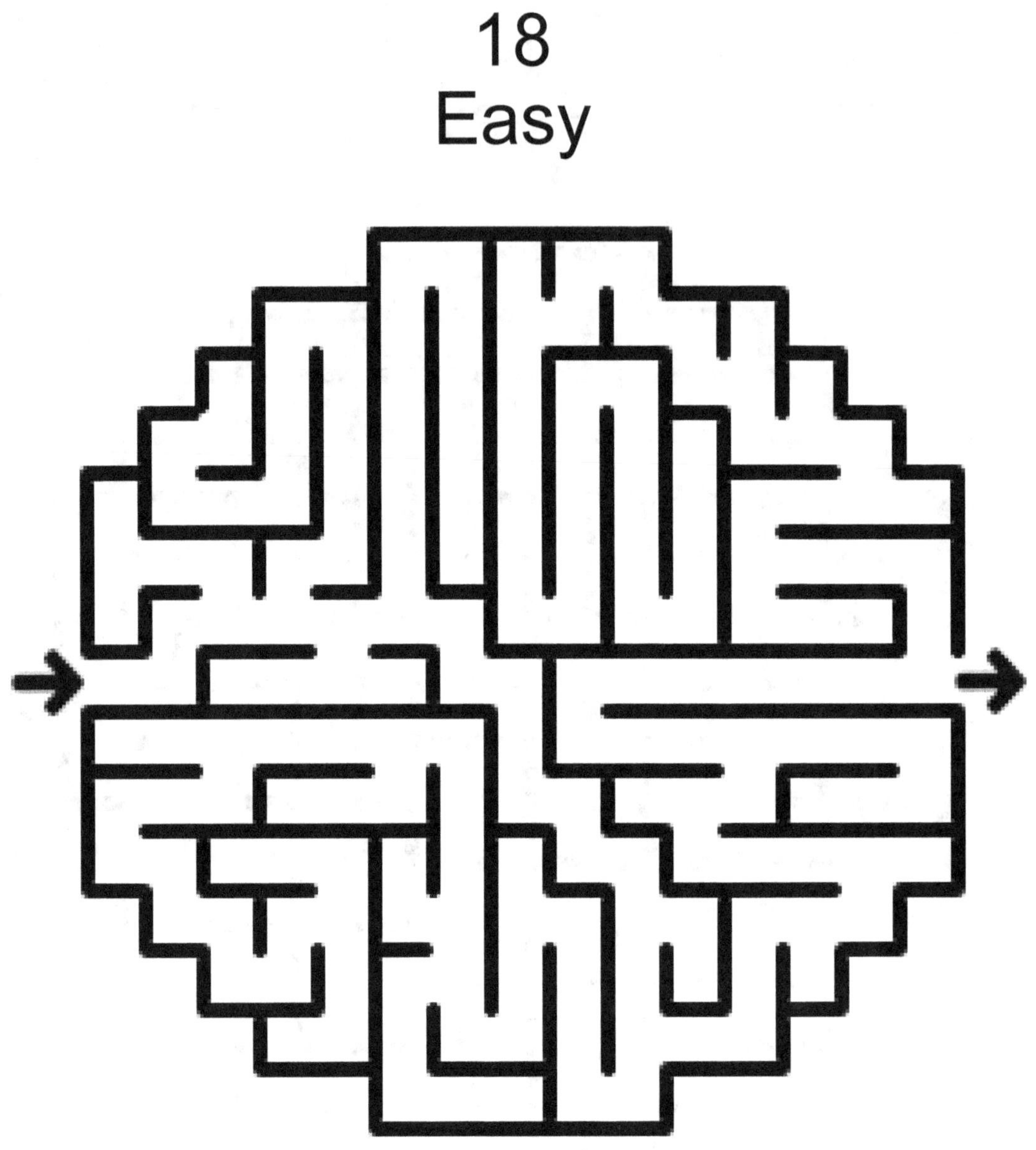

19
Easy

20
Easy

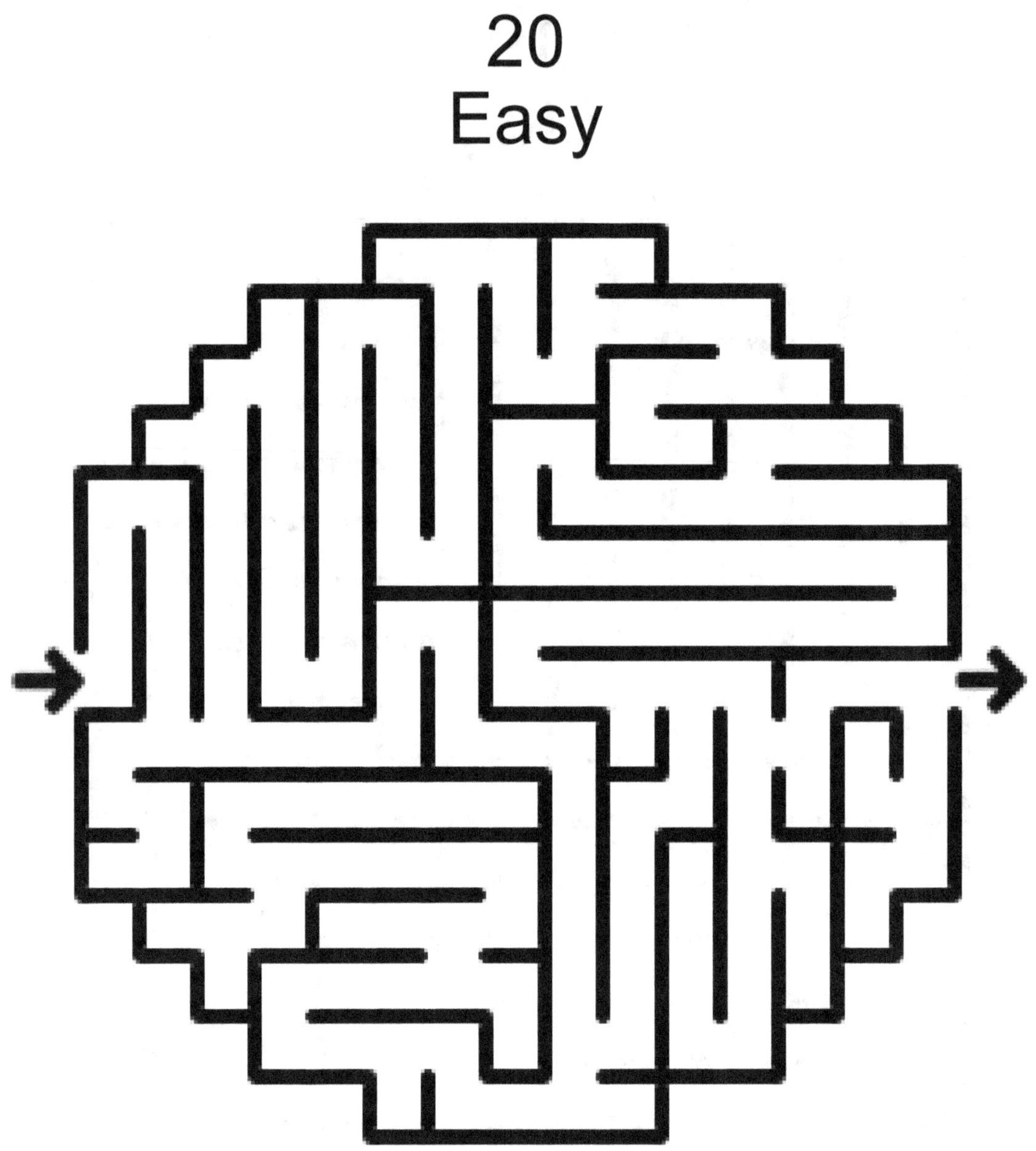

21
Easy – MEDIUM

22
Easy – MEDIUM

23
Easy – MEDIUM

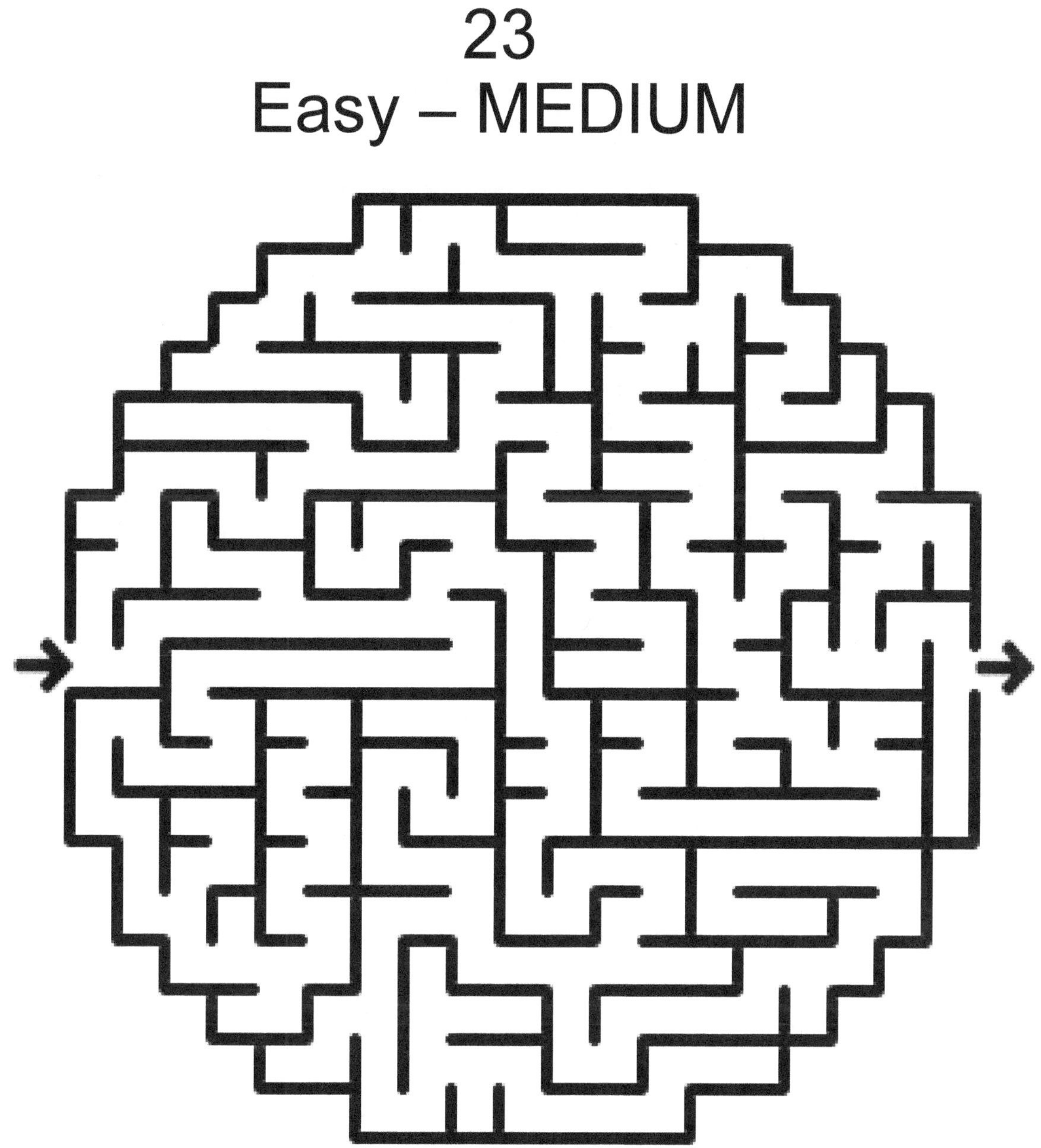

24
Easy – MEDIUM

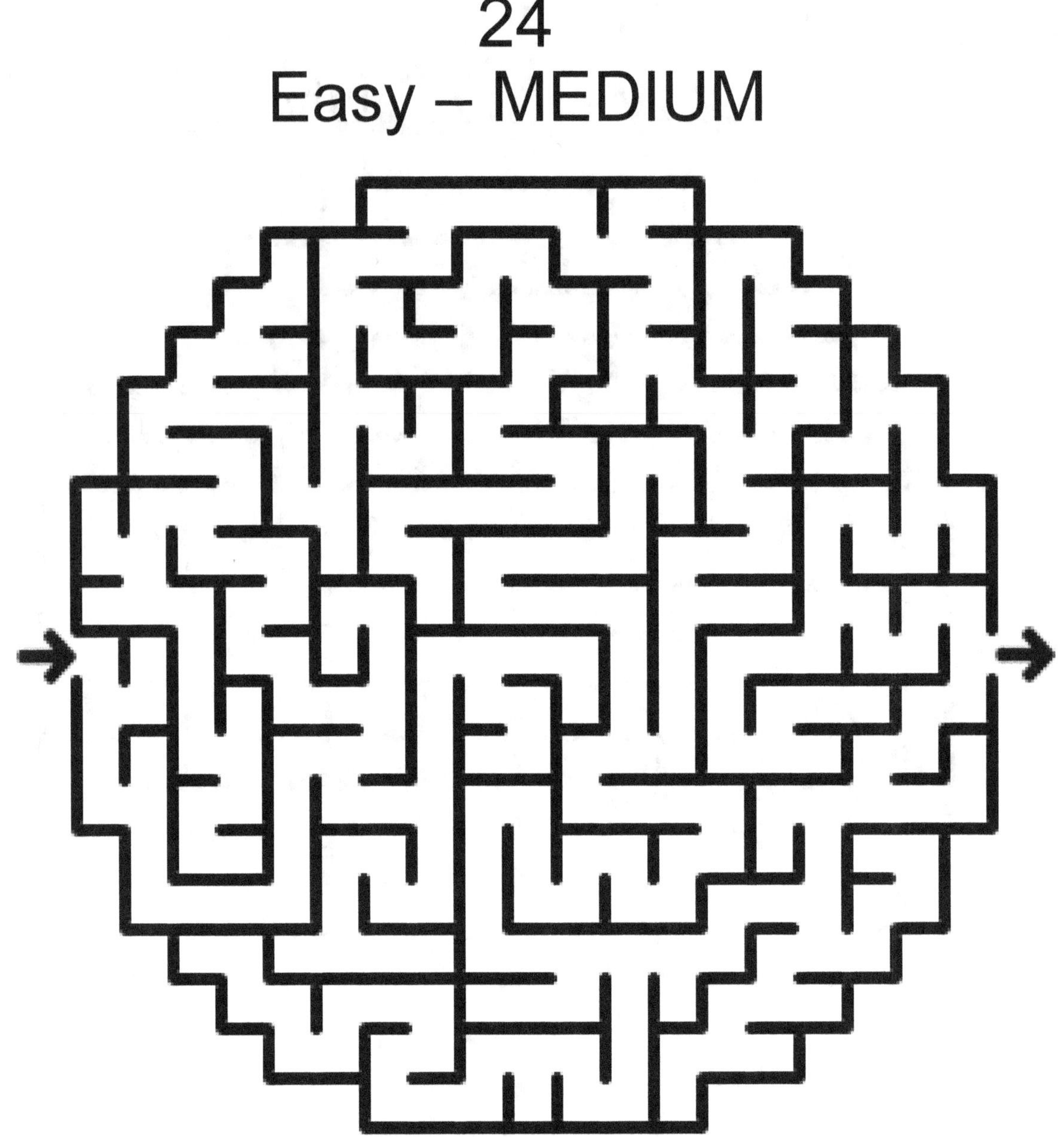

25
Easy – MEDIUM

26
Easy – MEDIUM

27
Easy – MEDIUM

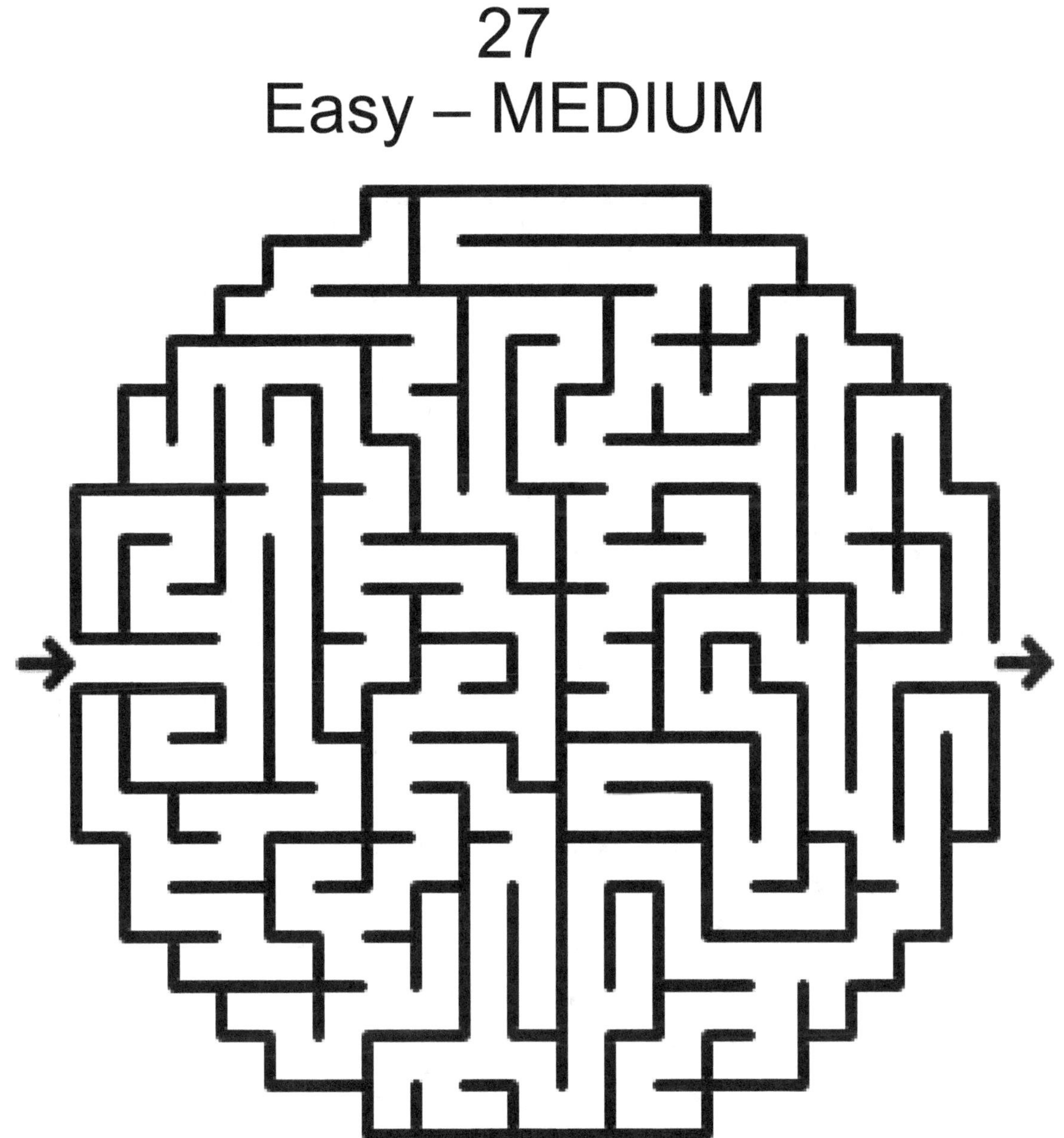

28
Easy – MEDIUM

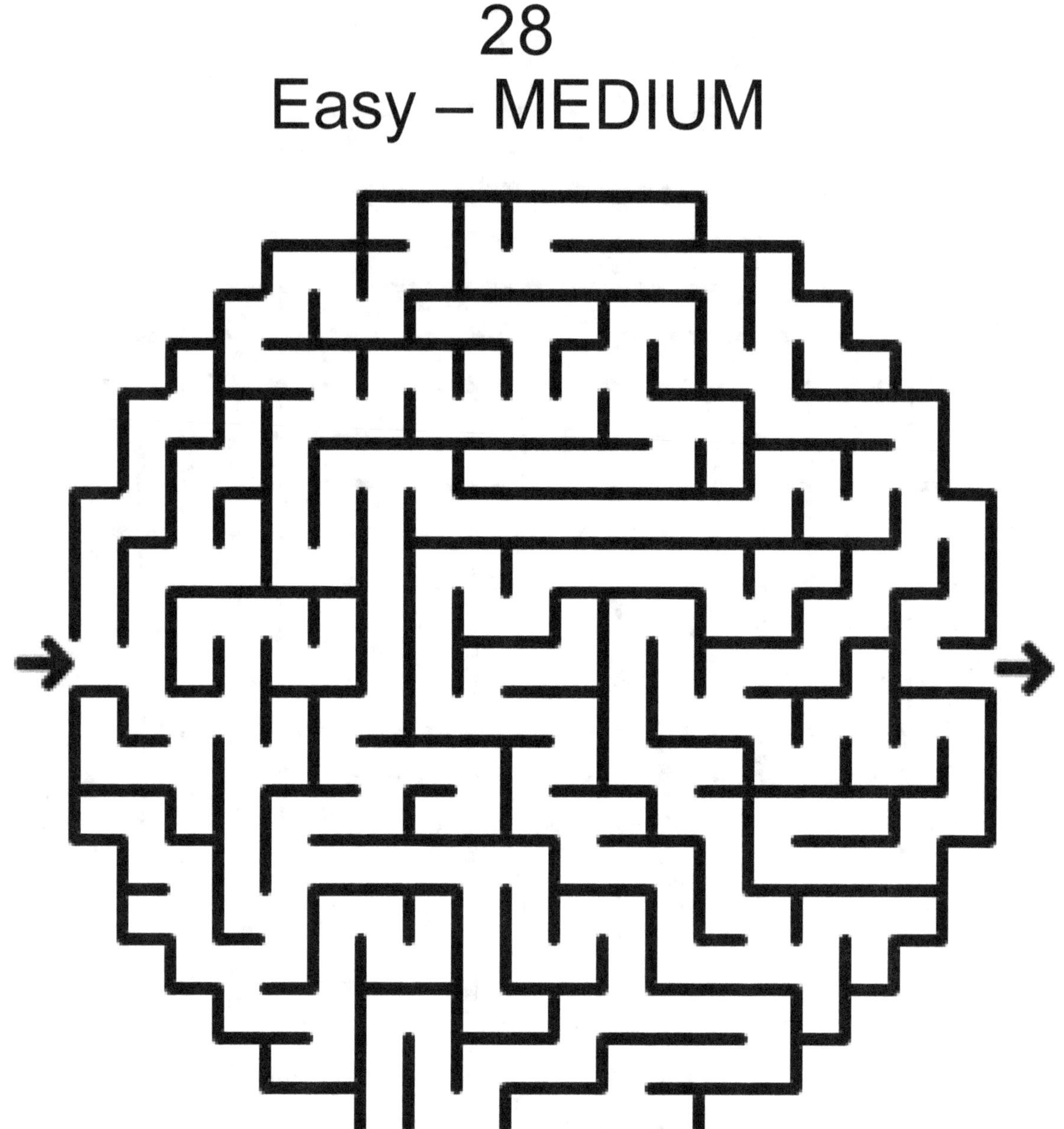

29
Easy – MEDIUM

30
Easy – MEDIUM

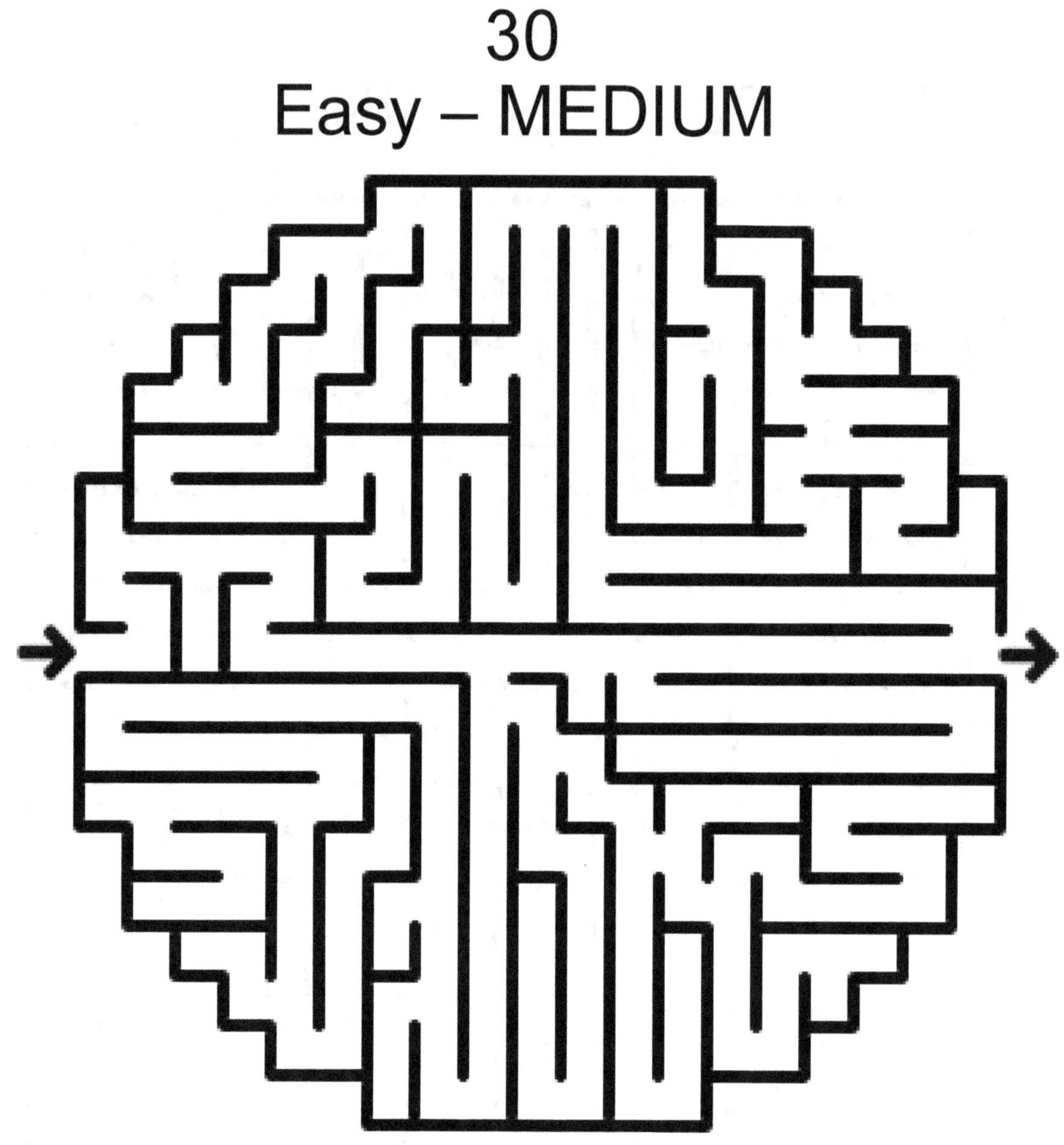

31
MEDIUM

32
MEDIUM

33
MEDIUM

34
MEDIUM

35
MEDIUM

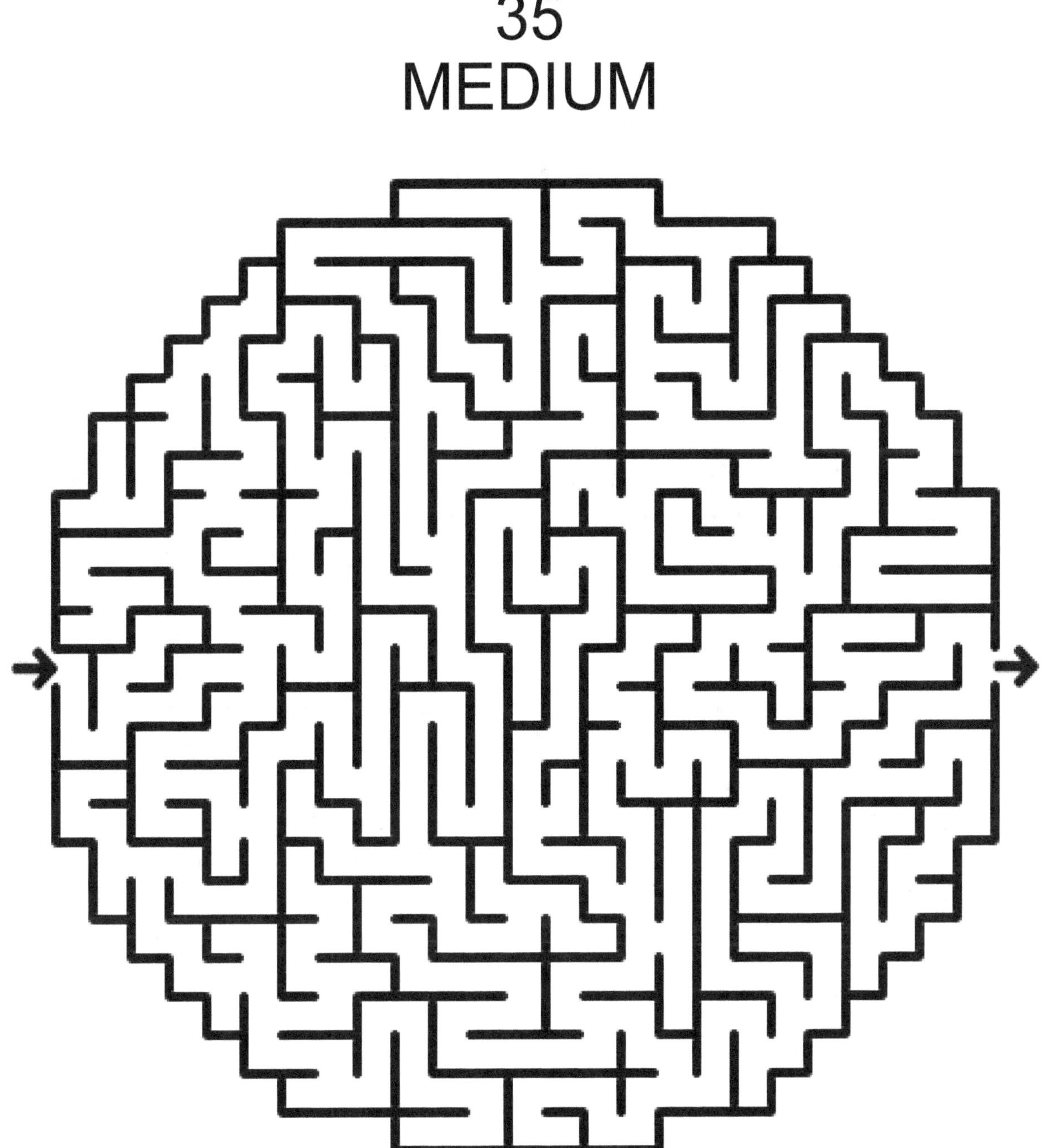

36
MEDIUM

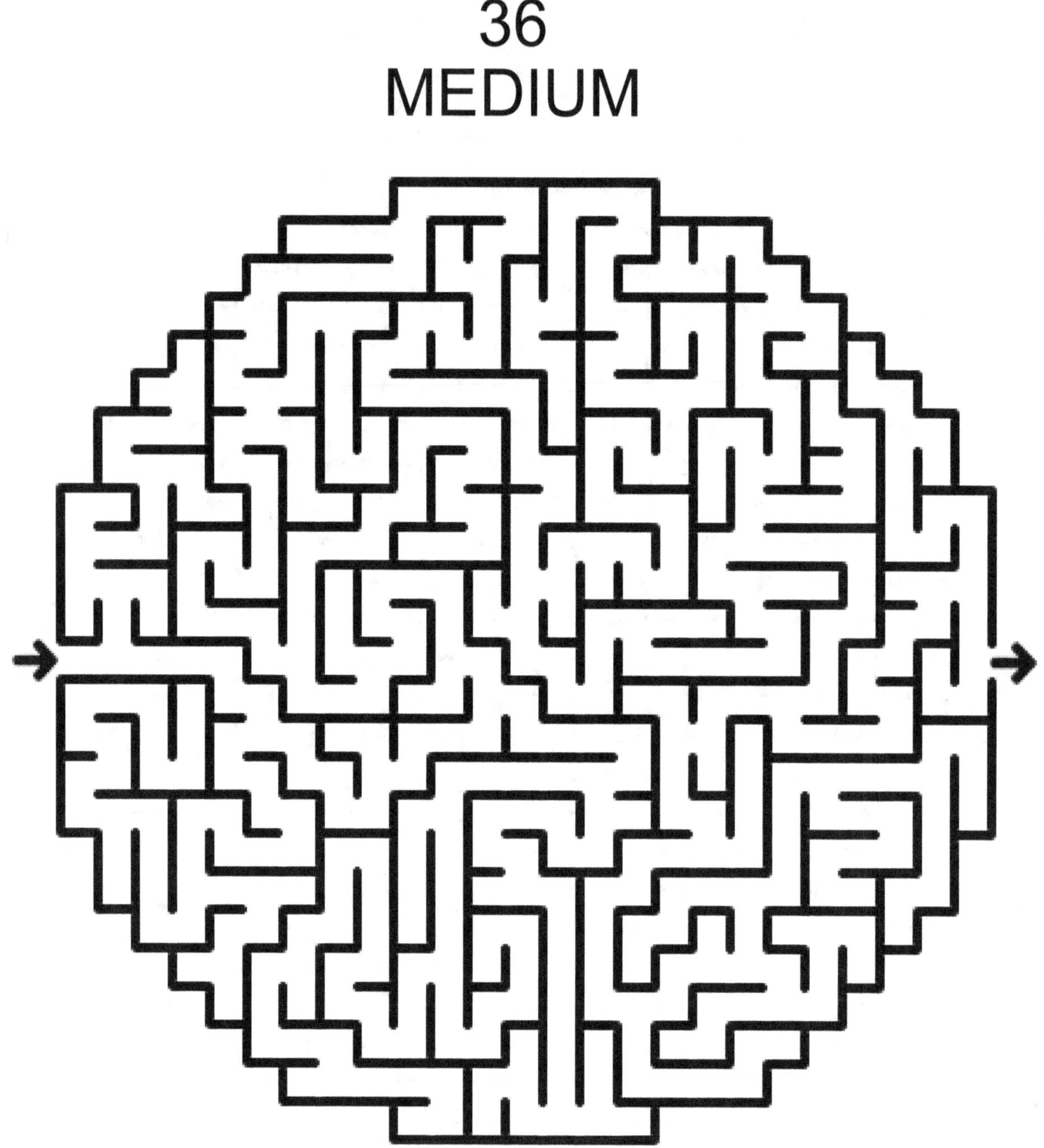

37
MEDIUM

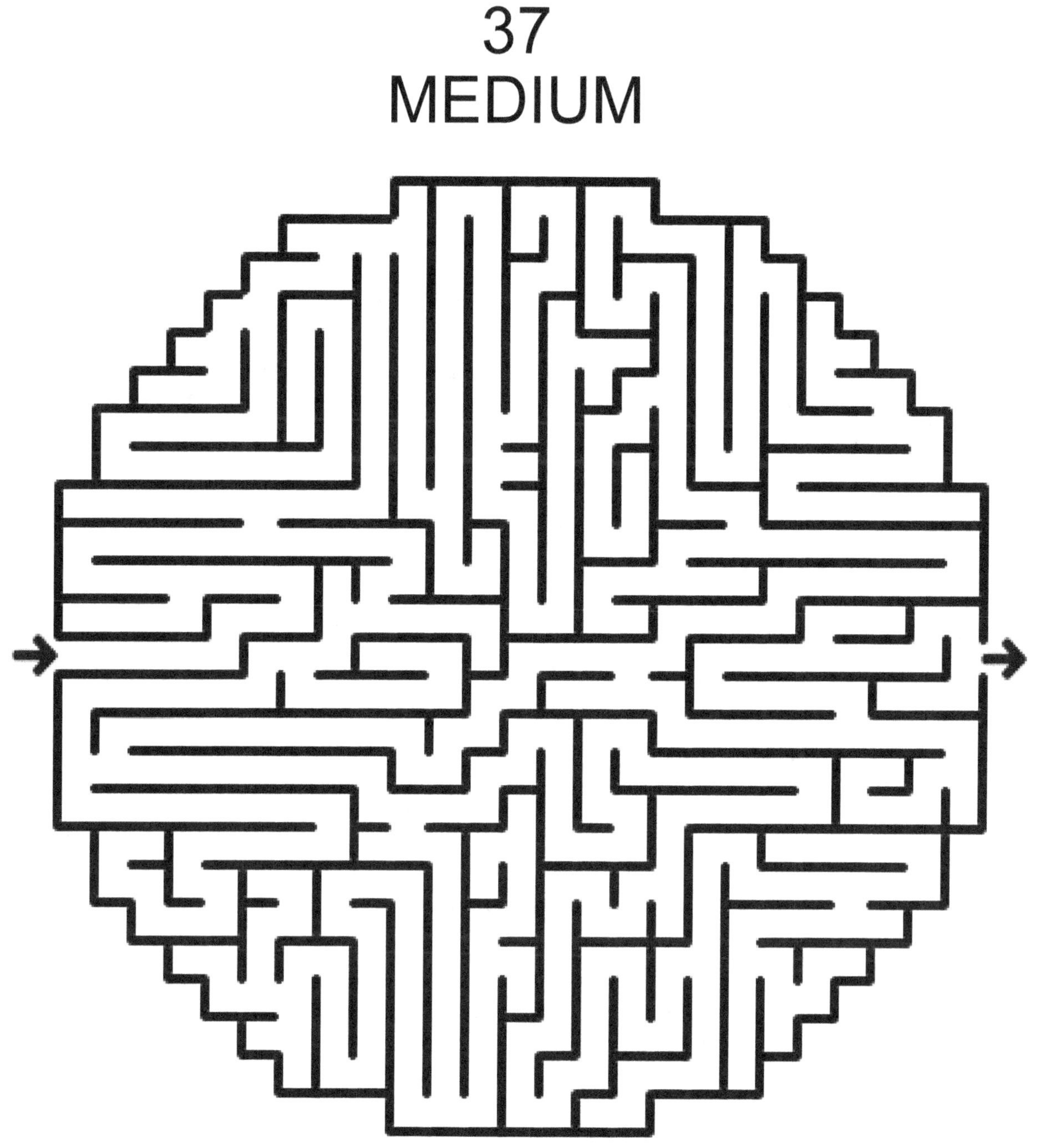

38
MEDIUM

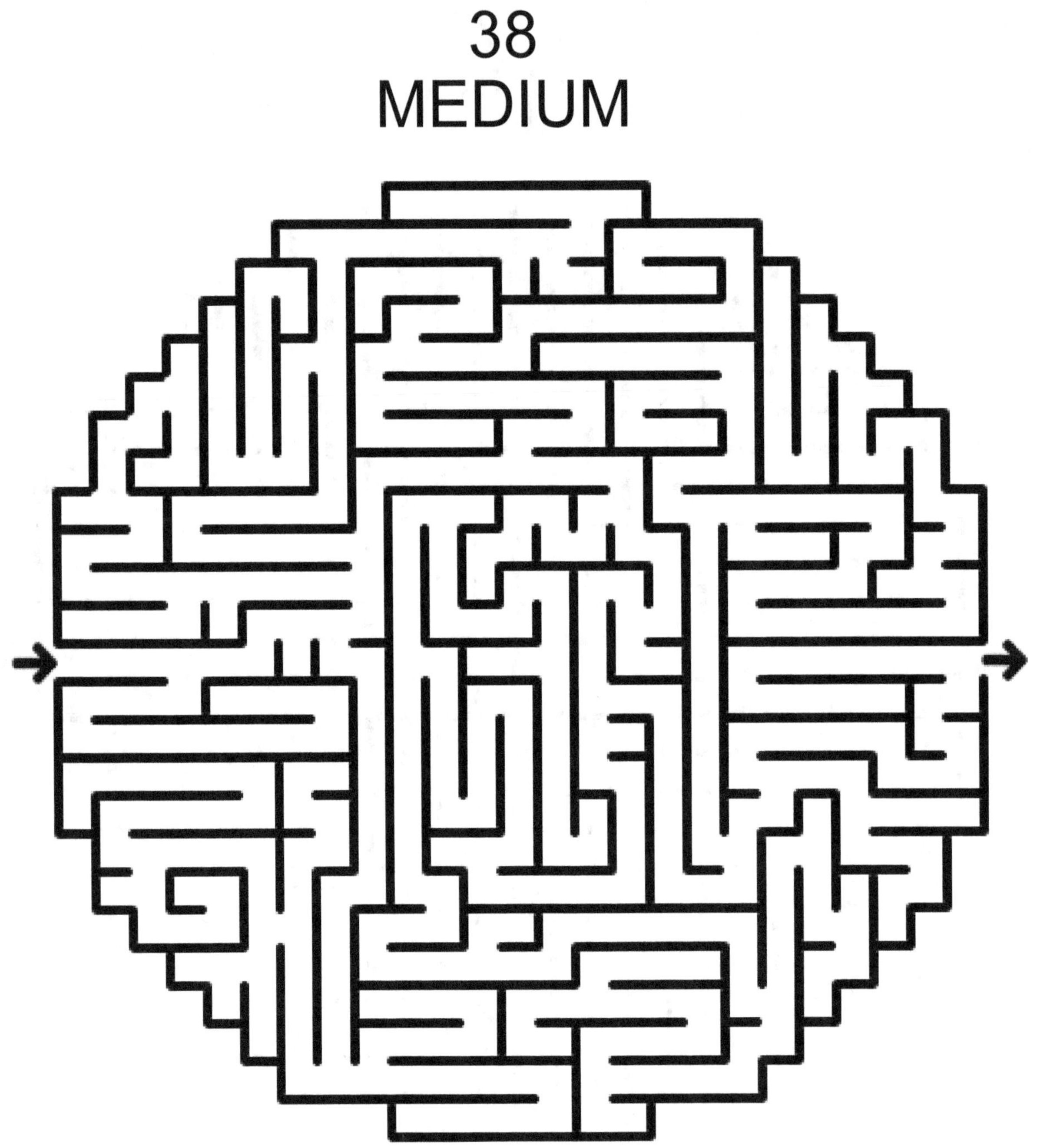

39
MEDIUM

40
MEDIUM

41
MEDIUM – DIFFICULT

42
MEDIUM – DIFFICULT

43
MEDIUM – DIFFICULT

44
MEDIUM – DIFFICULT

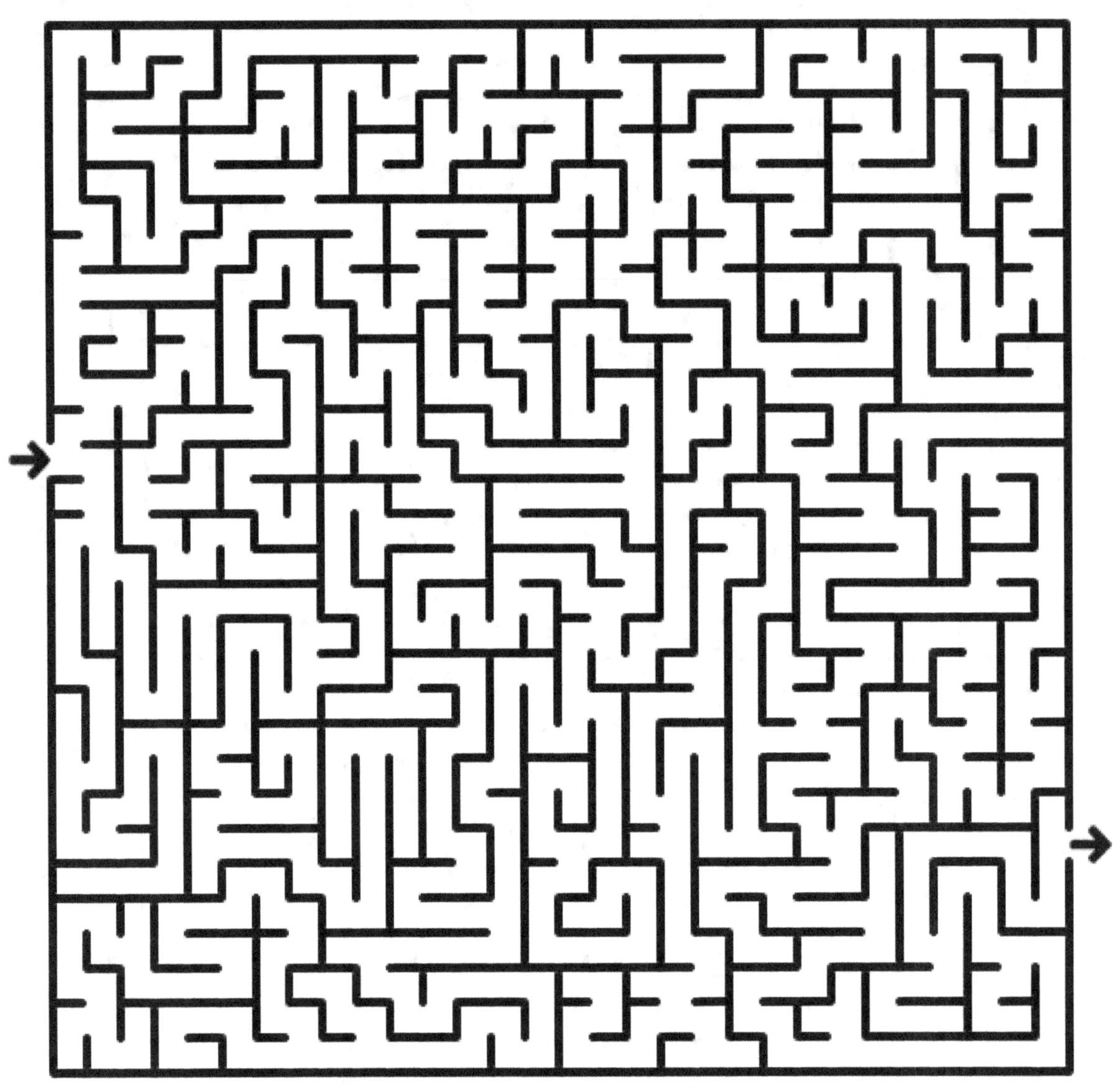

45
MEDIUM – DIFFICULT

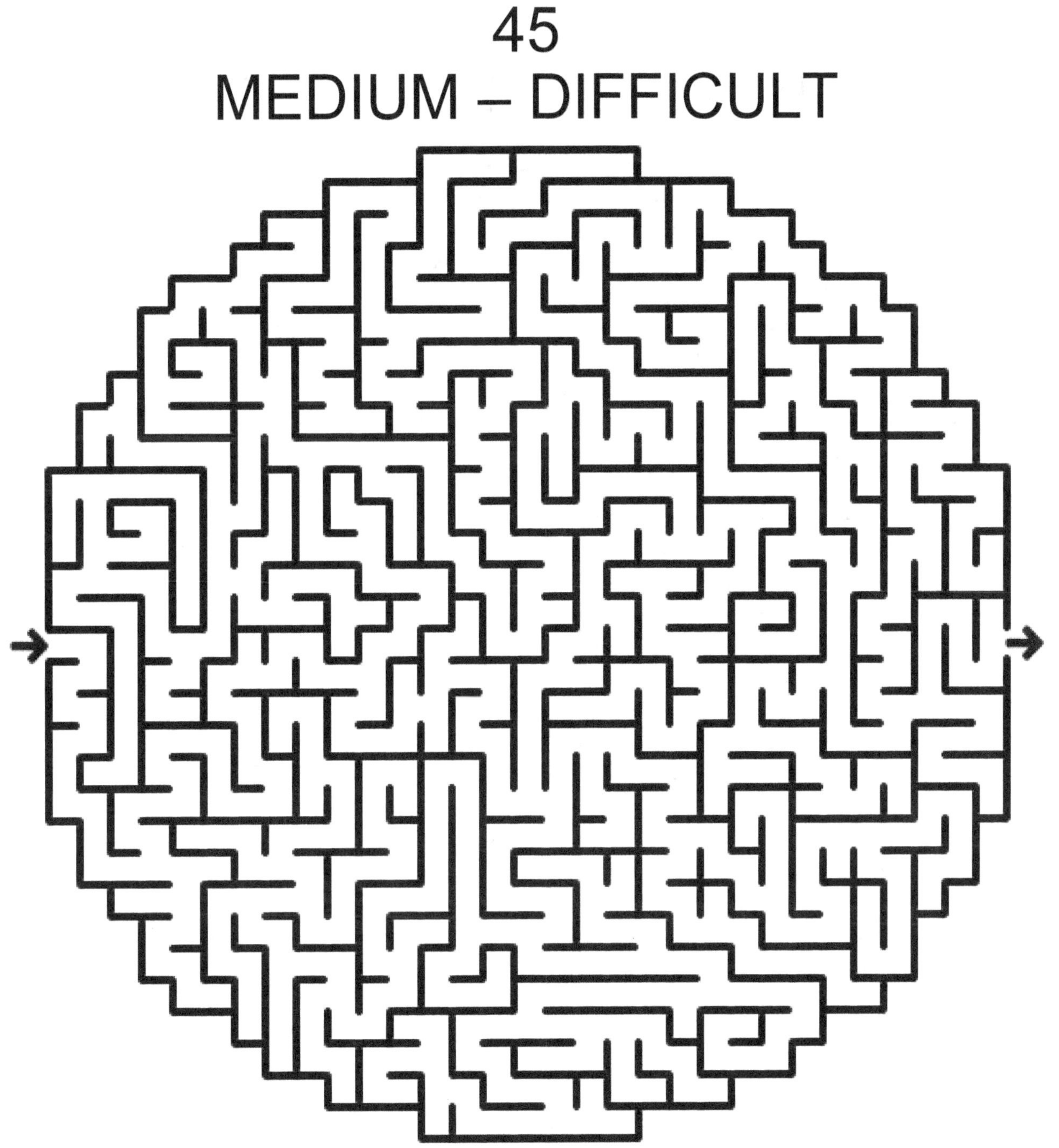

46
MEDIUM – DIFFICULT

47
MEDIUM – DIFFICULT

48
MEDIUM – DIFFICULT

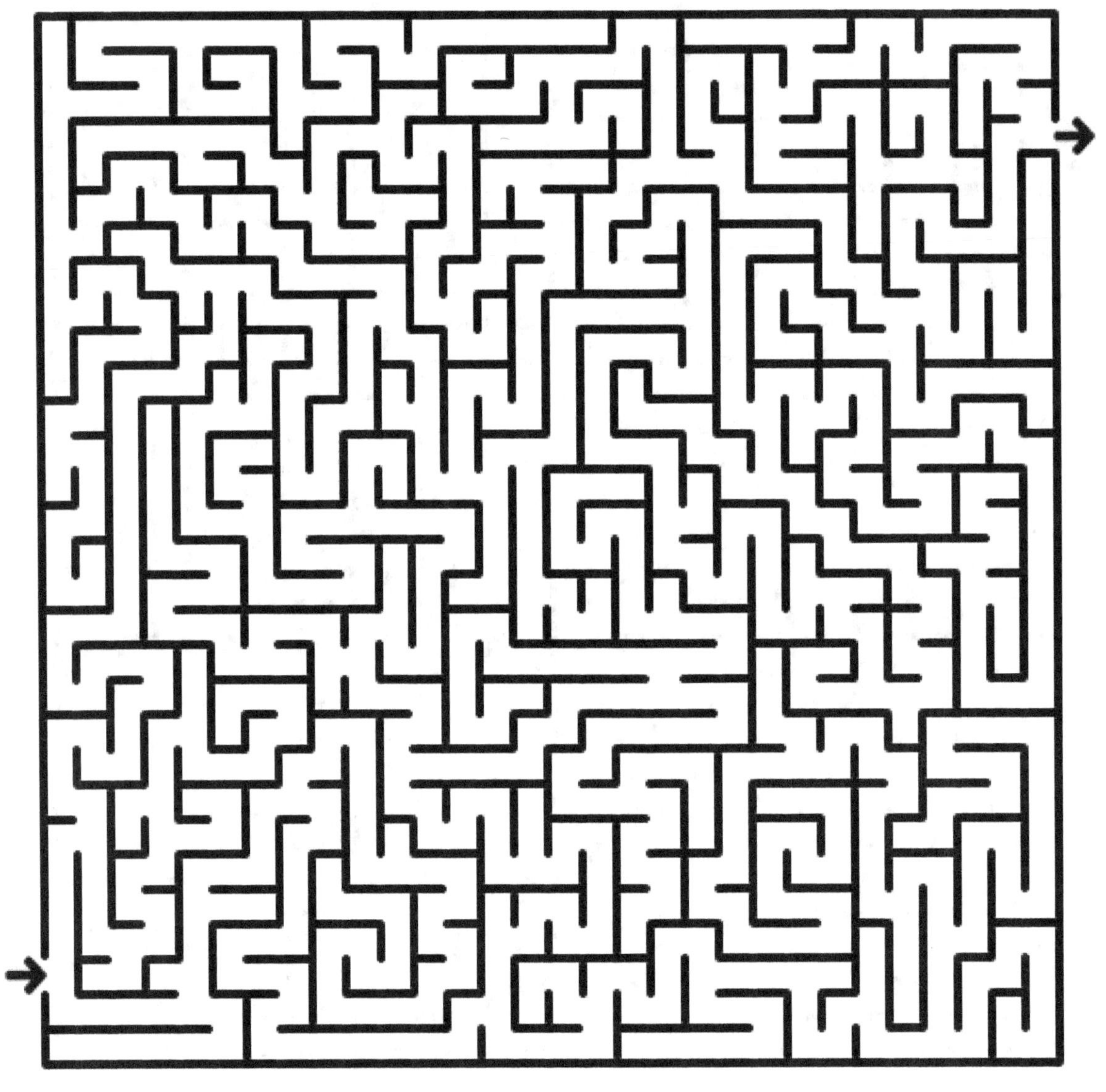

49
MEDIUM – DIFFICULT

50
MEDIUM – DIFFICULT

51
DIFFICULT

52
DIFFICULT

53
DIFFICULT

54
DIFFICULT

55
DIFFICULT

56
DIFFICULT

57
DIFFICULT

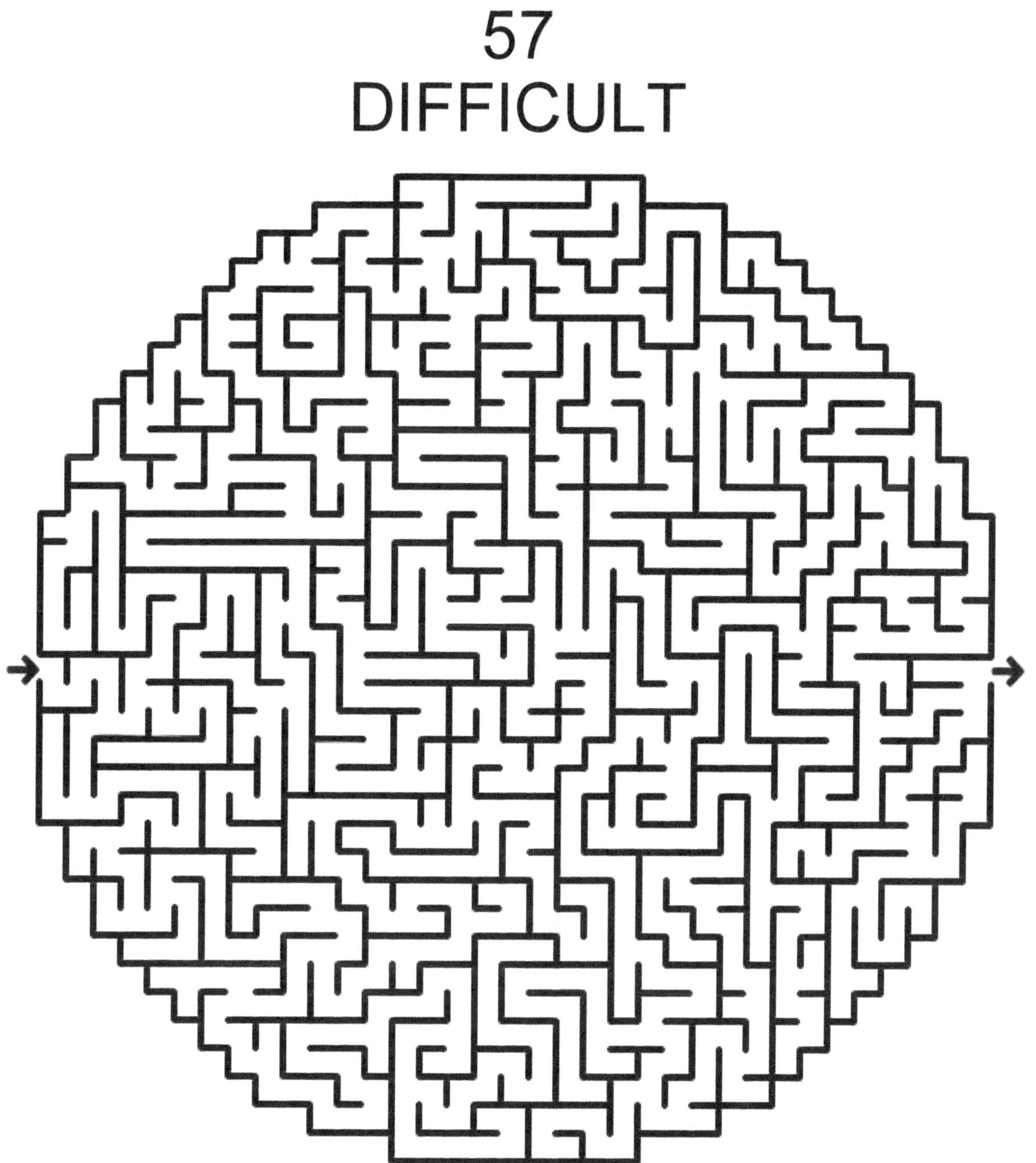

58
DIFFICULT

59
DIFFICULT

60
DIFFICULT

61
SUPER – DIFFICULT

62
SUPER – DIFFICULT

63
SUPER – DIFFICULT

64
SUPER – DIFFICULT

65
SUPER – DIFFICULT

66
SUPER – DIFFICULT

67
SUPER – DIFFICULT

68
SUPER – DIFFICULT

69
SUPER – DIFFICULT

70
SUPER – DIFFICULT

Name: _______________________________

Age: _______________________________

Notes

____

____

____

____

____

____

____

____

____

____

____

Also Available by the Same Authors:

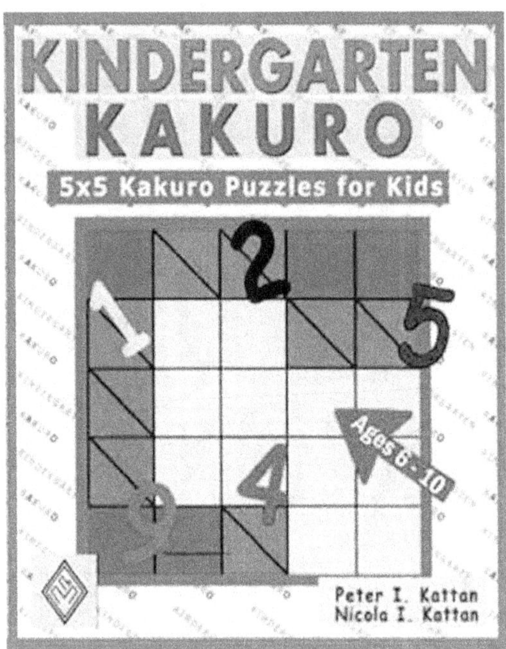

Level 1
Kindergarten
Puzzles
Ages 4 - 8
Simple Puzzles
A
B
C
D
1
2
3
4
Worksheets
Activities for Kids
Peter I. Kattan
Nicola I. Kattan

Level 2
Kindergarten
Puzzles
Ages 4 - 8
Simple Puzzles
O
P
Q
R
6
7
8
9
Worksheets
Activities for Kids
Peter I. Kattan
Nicola I. Kattan

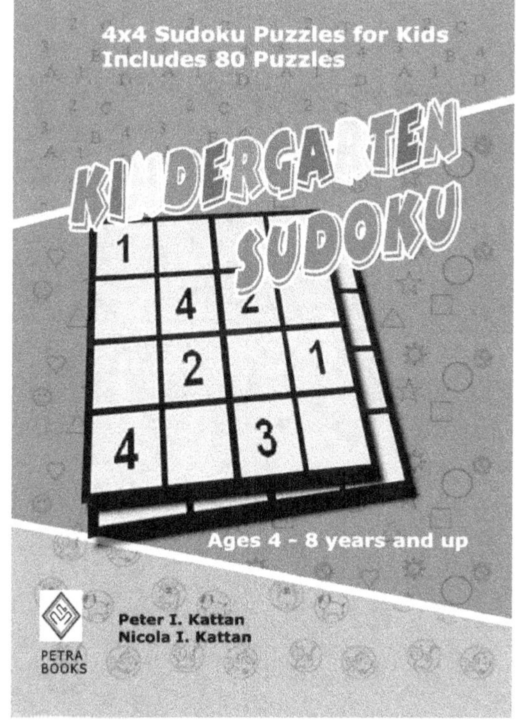
4x4 Sudoku Puzzles for Kids
Includes 80 Puzzles
KINDERGARTEN
SUDOKU
Ages 4 - 8 years and up
Peter I. Kattan
Nicola I. Kattan
PETRA BOOKS

MORE
KINDERGARTEN
SUDOKU
Ages 4 - 8 years and up
EASY
MEDIUM
DIFFICULT
4x4 Classic Sudoku Puzzles for Kids
Includes 96 Puzzles
Peter I. Kattan
Nicola I. Kattan